Contents

1. Continue the pattern.

50   60

25   35

42   52

2. Add

15 + 5 = ☐   12 + 6 = ☐   11 + 7 = ☐

17 + 2 = ☐   14 + 2 = ☐   16 + 4 = ☐

13 + 5 = ☐   19 + 1 = ☐   18 + 2 = ☐

3. How much?

= ☐ p   = ☐ p   = ☐ p   = ☐ p

4. Colour the hexagons.

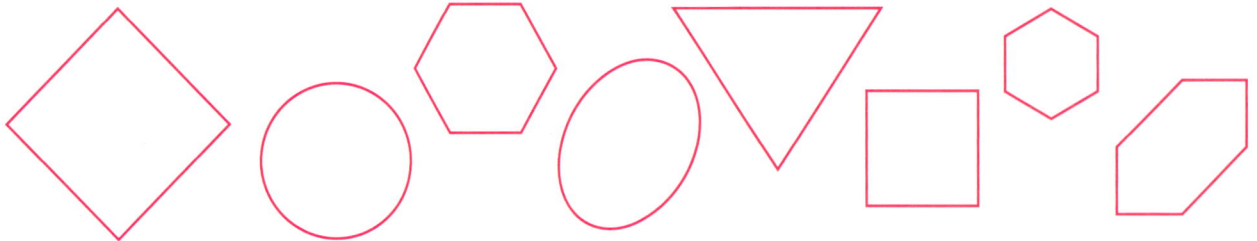

5. Write the numbers in order. ⑯46 ⑱48 ⑭44 ⑰47 ⑮45

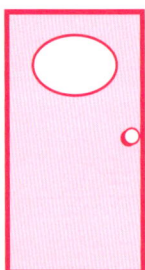 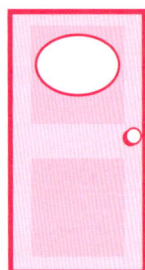  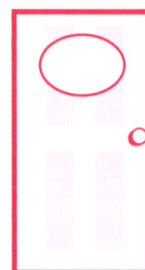 

Schofield&Sims

Mental Maths 2

Name

Schofield&Sims

Mental Maths Book 2
written by Anne Forster and Paul Martin

MENTAL MATHS is a series of two workbooks.

| Book One | 978 07217 0962 8 |
| Book Two | 978 07217 0963 5 |

Notes for the teacher

The purpose of this series of books is to encourage and develop mental agility in Mathematics at Key Stage I. Each book contains a series of structured exercises to carefully build children's confidence in their mathematical knowledge, interspersed with short progress tests. Each page provides a variety of tasks taken from different areas of the mathematics curriculum at Key Stage I. A wide range of vocabulary is used to introduce children to the variety of ways in which questions can be asked.

This book includes questions in the following key areas:

Number bonds, time, number sequences, fractions, money, measurement, times tables, pictorial and verbal problems, and shape.

First printed 2004

Twenty-third impression 2022

Printed in the UK by Page Bros (Norwich) Ltd

Design by www.ledgardjepson.com

1. Subtract

    20 – 3 = ☐   18 – 6 = ☐   12 – 6 = ☐

    14 – 2 = ☐   13 – 6 = ☐   15 – 6 = ☐

    17 – 5 = ☐   11 – 5 = ☐   19 – 8 = ☐

2. Write the next number.

    14 ◯   20 ◯   29 ◯   35 ◯   40 ◯   49 ◯

5. Write the time.

     $\frac{1}{4}$ to ☐   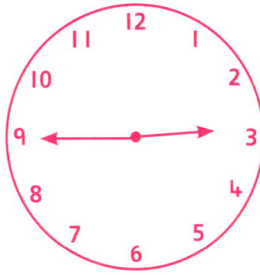 $\frac{1}{4}$ to ☐   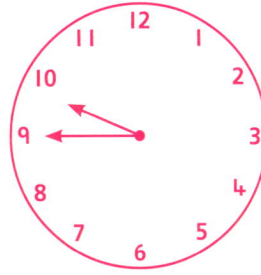 $\frac{1}{4}$ to ☐   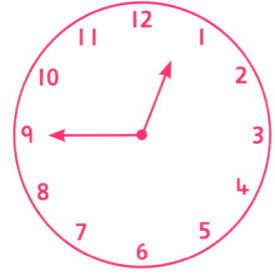 $\frac{1}{4}$ to ☐

4. Write ten more.

    10 → ☐   40 → ☐   60 → ☐   80 → ☐

    30 → ☐   70 → ☐   50 → ☐   90 → ☐

5. Mary had 15 daisies in her daisy chain.

    She added 4 more daisies.

    Then she had ◯ daisies in her daisy chain.

    Joe paid 20p for a cornet 🍦 and 5p for a lollipop 🍭.

    He spent   = ☐ p

1. Write the months of the year in order.

August   May   November   January

February   December   October   April   June

September   July   March

1. _____   2. _____   3. _____

4. _____   5. _____   6. _____

7. _____   8. _____   9. _____

10. _____   11. _____   12. _____

2. Add and Take

15 + 3 – 5 = ☐   20 + 0 – 5 = ☐   17 + 2 – 3 = ☐

14 + 5 – 6 = ☐   13 + 3 – 6 = ☐   12 + 8 – 3 = ☐

3. Circle the largest number in each shape.

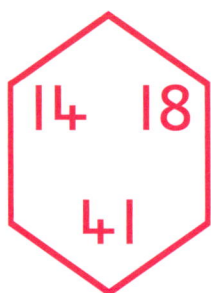

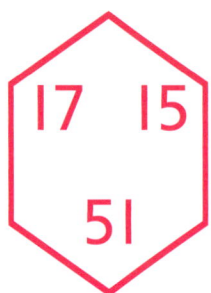

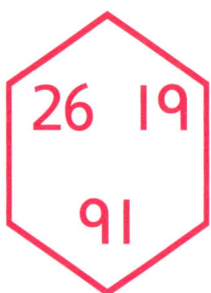

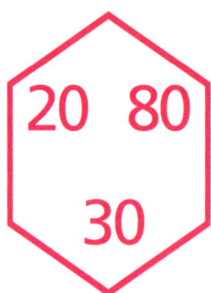

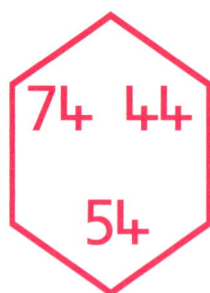

14 18   17 15   26 19   20 80   74 44
  41   51   91   30   54

4. Colour the cylinders.

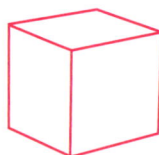

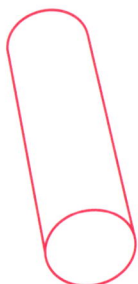

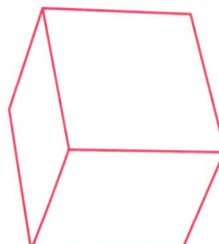

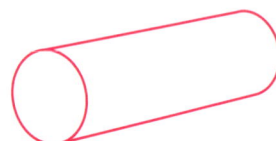

Progress Test A

1. Continue the pattern.

46 47 48 ◯ ◯ ◯ ◯

48 49 50 ◯ ◯ ◯ ◯

65 66 67 ◯ ◯ ◯ ◯

2. Write the numbers for the words.

twenty ☐ twenty-one ☐

forty ☐ fifty-five ☐

thirty-seven ☐ forty-nine ☐

3. Name the coin.

= ☐ p = ☐

4. Find the missing number to make 50.

 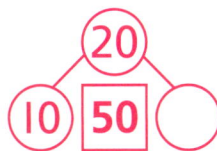

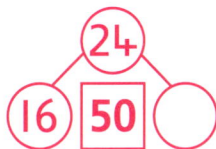 

5. Estimate how long the rope is. Write your answer in cm.

☐ cm

6. Write the number before.

⬡ 21 ⬡ 29 ⬡ 30

⬡ 37 ⬡ 40 ⬡ 48

7. Write these months in order.

June   January   July

_____

_____

_____

8. Make each purse hold 30p.

9. Add and Take

16 + 4 − 10 = ☐   27 + 2 − 10 = ☐

25 + 2 − 5 = ☐   21 + 9 − 8 = ☐

19 + 3 − 4 = ☐   30 + 3 − 0 = ☐

10. What time is it?

 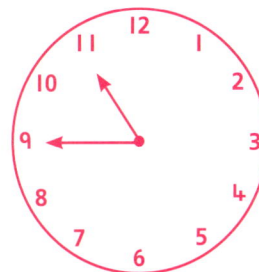

$\frac{1}{4}$ to ☐ $\frac{1}{4}$ to ☐

1. 10 less

70 ☐ 30 ☐ 50 ☐ 80 ☐ 100 ☐

32 ☐ 65 ☐ 89 ☐ 48 ☐ 96 ☐

2. Circle the smallest number in each shape.

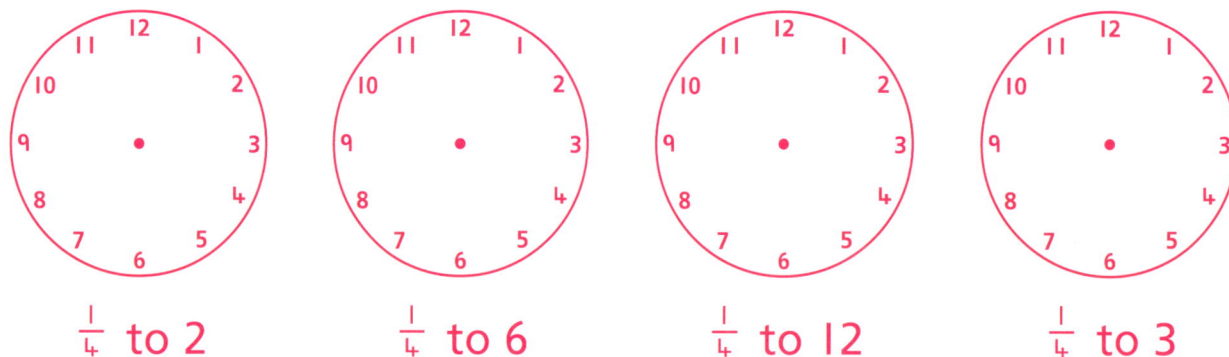

| 38 30 | 59 60 | 92 87 | 93 99 | 90 89 |
| 29 | 63 | 77 | 97 | 100 |

3. Draw the hands on the clocks.

$\frac{1}{4}$ to 2 $\frac{1}{4}$ to 6 $\frac{1}{4}$ to 12 $\frac{1}{4}$ to 3

4. Find the missing number.

$10 = 6 +$ ☐ $8 = 4 +$ ☐ $9 = 3 +$ ☐

$15 = 10 +$ ☐ $19 = 9 +$ ☐ $12 = 6 +$ ☐

☐ $= 15 + 4$ ☐ $= 6 + 7$ ☐ $= 11 + 9$

5. How much change from 50p?

 40p    20p    30p

I had ☐ p   I had ☐ p   I had ☐ p
change.   change.   change.

1. Use 3 coins to make 50p.

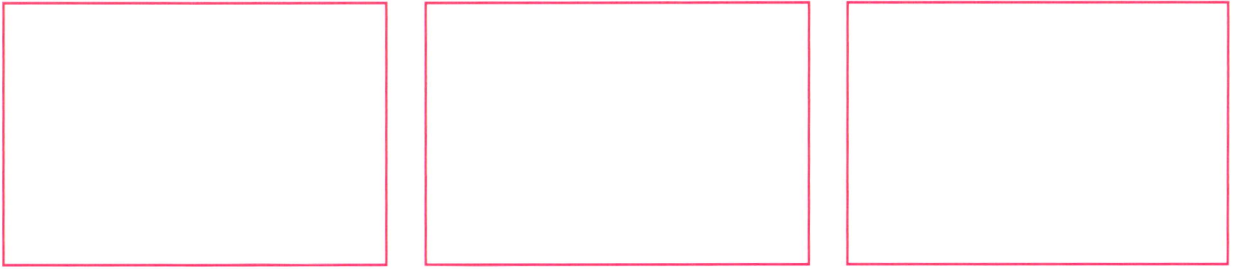

2. Add

$15 + 20 =$ ☐ $17 + 10 =$ ☐ $32 + 8 =$ ☐

$22 + 5 =$ ☐ $30 + 15 =$ ☐ $18 + 22 =$ ☐

$25 + 15 =$ ☐ $36 + 12 =$ ☐ $25 + 25 =$ ☐

3. Colour the octagons.

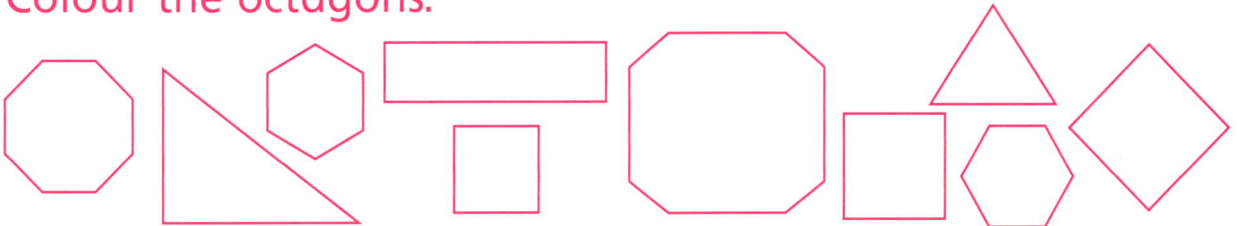

4. Write the numbers on the buses in order. 89 91 90 98 92

lowest   highest

5. The buses are running 1 hour late. Show the time 1 hour later.

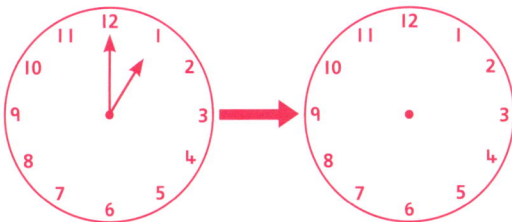

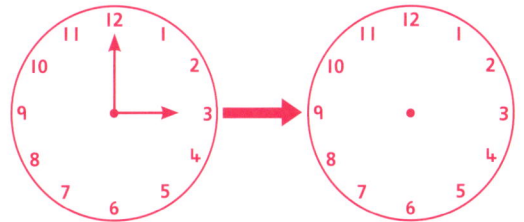

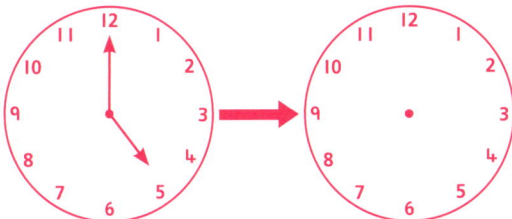

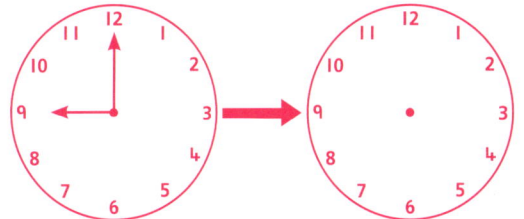

1. Write the number after.

25 ◯　29 ◯　40 ◯　38 ◯　49 ◯

2. Match the sums to the answers.

25 + 24

22 + 15

11 + 33

50　44
46　　　49
47　37

36 + 11

44 + 6

21 + 25

3. Double the numbers.

20 → ☐　30 → ☐　40 → ☐　50 → ☐

4. Draw the beads on each abacus.

21 =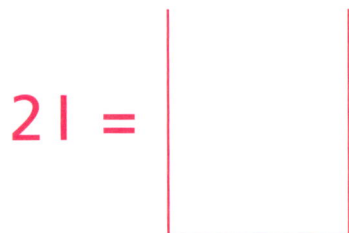
Tens　Ones

35 =
Tens　Ones

37 =
Tens　Ones

50 =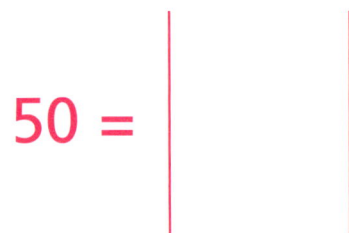
Tens　Ones

59 =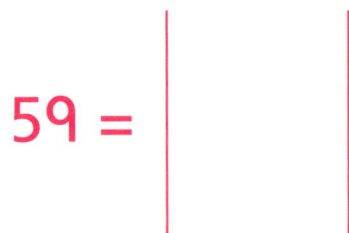
Tens　Ones

72 =
Tens　Ones

5. 38 plus 2 = ☐　19 add 20 = ☐　15 plus 45 = ☐

25 and 35 = ☐　48 and 13 = ☐　10 more than 66 = ☐

10

Progress Test B

1. 11 more than.

25 ⬡ 27 ⬡ 29 ⬡

32 ⬡ 40 ⬡ 35 ⬡

2. Draw the hands on the clocks.

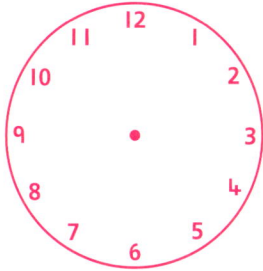 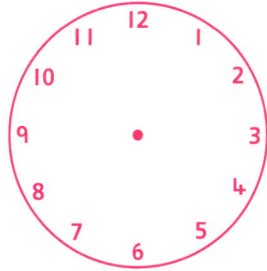

$\frac{1}{4}$ to 9 $\frac{1}{4}$ to 7

3. How many?

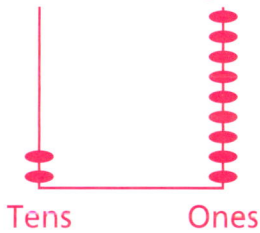 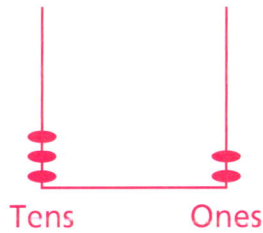

Tens   Ones   Tens   Ones

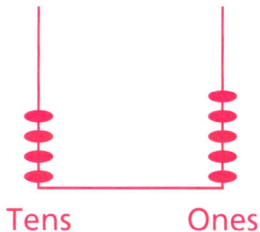 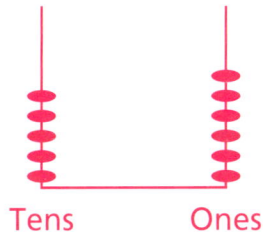

Tens   Ones   Tens   Ones

4. Draw a hexagon.

5. Make 60p in each box.

6. Write 5 numbers less than 50.

◯ ◯ ◯ ◯ ◯

7. Draw the beads on the abacus.

27 = 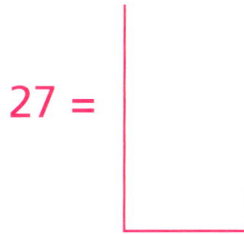   45 =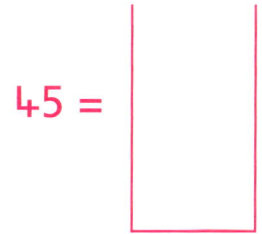

Tens   Ones   Tens   Ones

8. Match the trees to add up to 30.

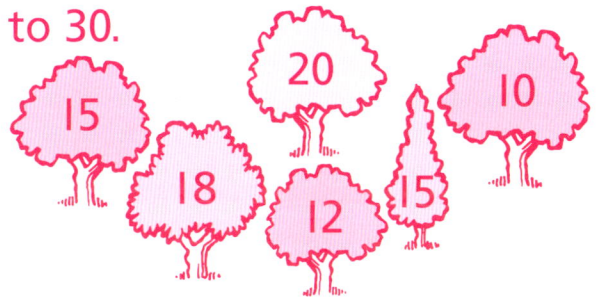

9. Draw the hands 1 hour later.

 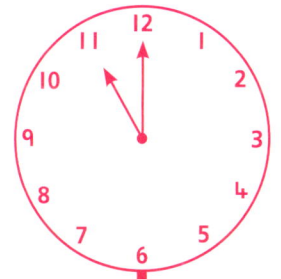

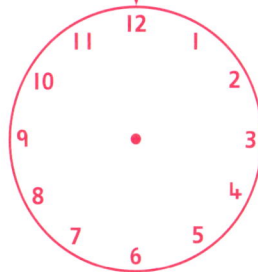 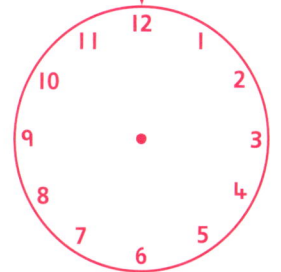

10. Draw 3 coins to make 35p.

11

1. Add

25 + 22 = ☐   17 + 15 = ☐   18 + 29 = ☐

37 + 14 = ☐   26 + 14 = ☐   32 + 19 = ☐

35 + 21 = ☐   18 + 19 = ☐   29 + 18 = ☐

2. Write the time.

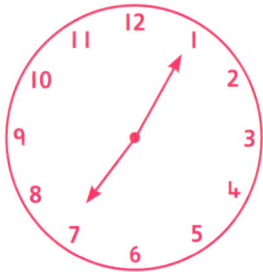
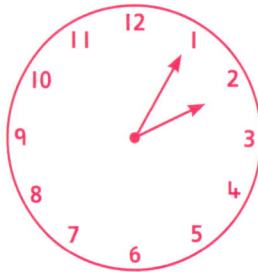
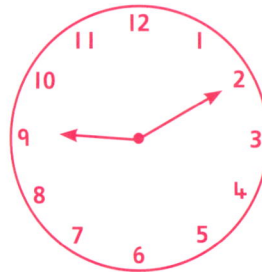
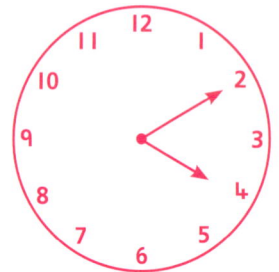

☐ past ☐   ☐ past ☐   ☐ past ☐   ☐ past ☐

3. Shopping

 10p
 15p
 31p
 25p

 15p
 45p
 5p
 16p

Colour blue 2 items of clothing that together cost 25p.
Colour red 2 items of clothing that together cost 50p.
Colour yellow 2 items of clothing that together cost 40p.
Colour green 2 items of clothing that together cost 47p.

4. Colour the pyramids.

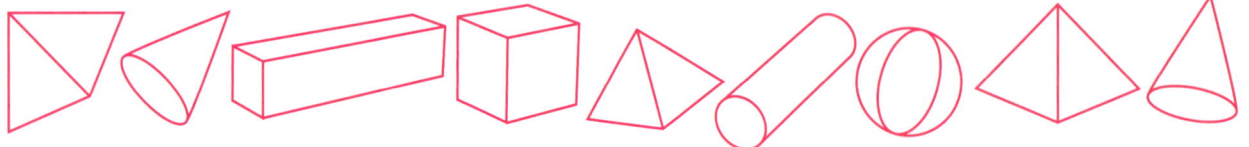

5. Continue the pattern.

1. Join the pairs of birds whose numbers add up to 50.

15　　9　　22　　19　　28　　35　　31　　41

2. Finish the bills.

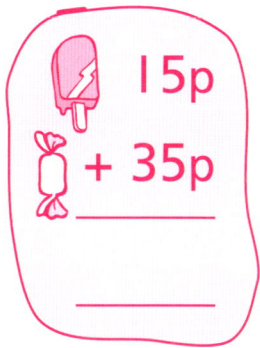

	15p
	+ 35p
	_____

	27p
	+ 18p
	_____

	18p
	+ 22p
	_____

	26p
	+ 24p
	_____

3. Put the clocks back 1 hour.

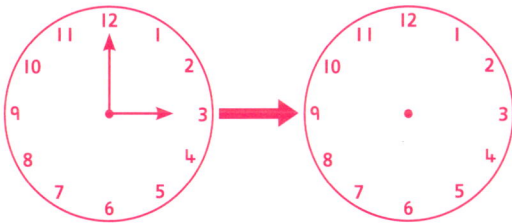

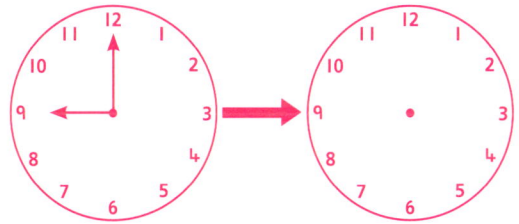

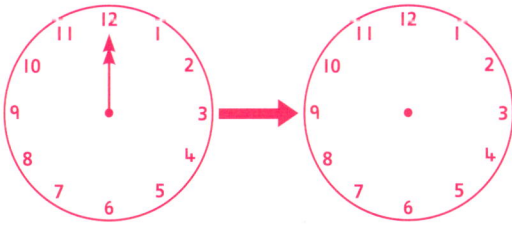

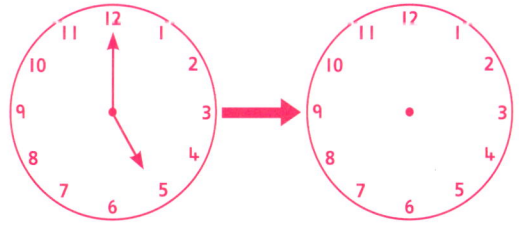

4. 20 less

35 ☐　　42 ☐　　21 ☐　　84 ☐

29 ☐　　65 ☐　　98 ☐　　100 ☐

5. Continue the patterns.

25　35　45　○　○　○　○

16　26　36　○　○　○　○

1. Count in 10s. Fill in the missing numbers.

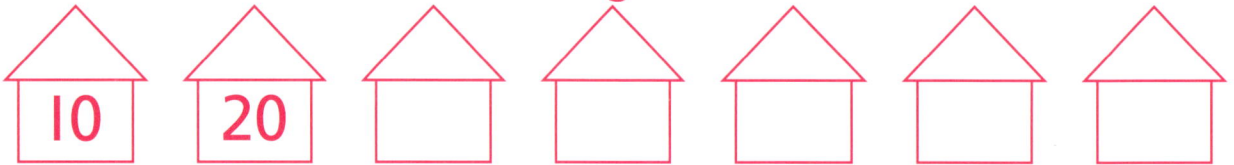

10 20 ☐ ☐ ☐ ☐ ☐

2. Multiply by 10

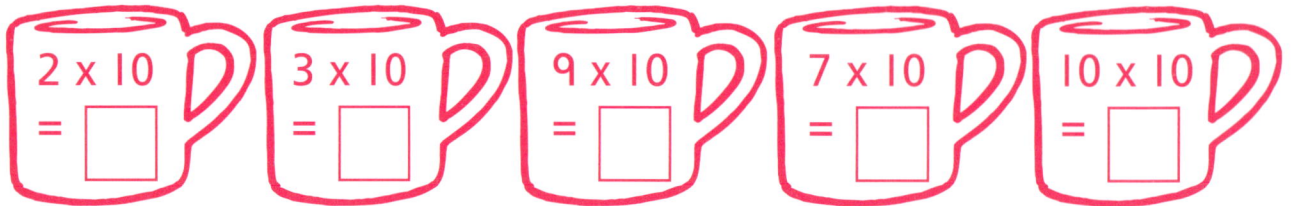

2 x 10 = ☐   3 x 10 = ☐   9 x 10 = ☐   7 x 10 = ☐   10 x 10 = ☐

3. Fill in the missing numbers.

24 + ☐ = 46   17 + ☐ = 25   21 + ☐ = 35

19 + ☐ = 28   11 + ☐ = 41   31 + ☐ = 50

☐ + 12 = 34   ☐ + 30 = 48   ☐ + 25 = 50

4. Write the number between.

29 ⬡ 31   38 ⬡ 40   44 ⬡ 46   48 ⬡ 50

5. Favourite Pets

dogs

mice

rabbits

cats

Which is the favourite pet?

_____

How many more children liked dogs than cats? ☐

How many more children liked rabbits than mice? ☐

14

Progress Test C

1. Fill in the missing numbers.

   2　4　6　◯ ◯ ◯ ◯

   10　12　14　◯ ◯ ◯ ◯

2. Join the bees that add up to 45.

3. Make the clocks show 1 hour earlier.

   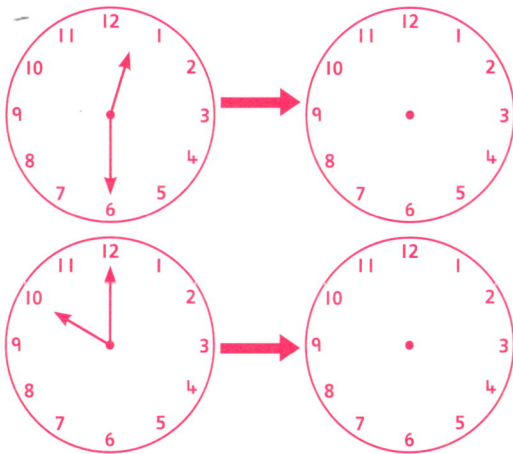

4. How much more to make 45p?

   [ ] p　　[ ] p　　[ ] p

5. Name the month after

   April＿＿＿＿　　January＿＿＿＿

   November＿＿＿＿　June ＿＿＿＿

6. Use these numbers to make the following sums.

   ⑩　⑫　㉕　㉚

   [ ] + [ ] = 37　　[ ] + [ ] = 35

   [ ] + [ ] = 22　　[ ] + [ ] = 42

7. How much?

   [ ] p　　[ ] p　　[ ] p

8. Write the time.

   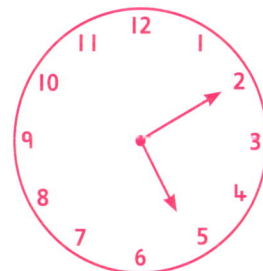 

   [ ] past [ ]　　[ ] past [ ]

9. Draw a pyramid.

10. Multiply by 10

   6 x 10 = [ ]　　7 x 10 = [ ]

   8 x 10 = [ ]　　4 x 10 = [ ]

1. Colour $\frac{3}{4}$ of each shape.

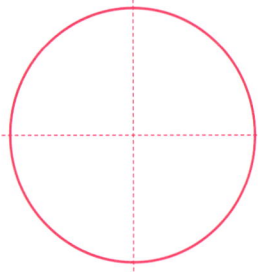

2. Add

75 + 20 = ☐   50 + 25 = ☐   15 + 34 = ☐

28 + 41 = ☐   62 + 34 = ☐   73 + 16 = ☐

38 + 22 = ☐   54 + 46 = ☐   35 + 64 = ☐

3. Use these digits to write the largest numbers you can.

2, 6 (62)   4, 3 ◯   1, 9 ◯   2, 3 ◯

7, 8 ◯   8, 9 ◯   0, 7 ◯   9, 5 ◯

4. Colour the spheres.

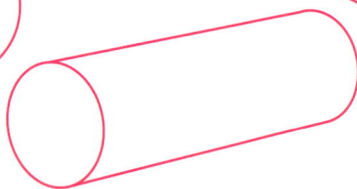

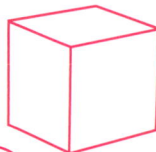

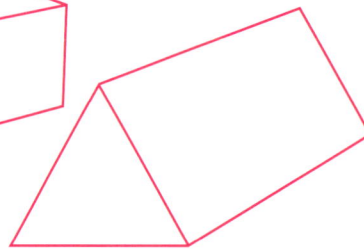

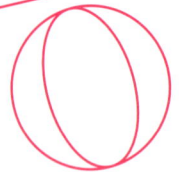

5. How many 10s in...?

20 ☐   50 ☐   70 ☐

90 ☐   32 ☐   45 ☐

1. Add

20 + 30 = ☐   70 + 20 = ☐   50 + 40 = ☐

40 + 40 = ☐   80 + 10 = ☐   10 + 30 = ☐

90 + 10 = ☐   60 + 30 = ☐   50 + 50 = ☐

2. Write the time.

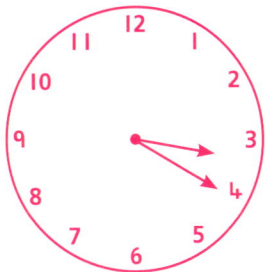   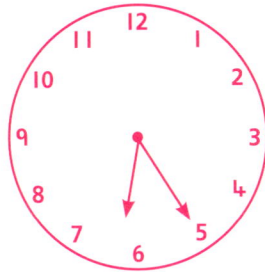   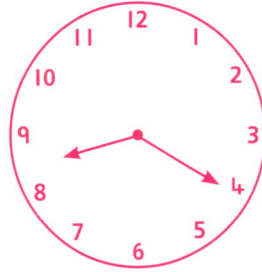   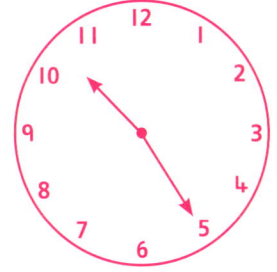

20 past ☐   25 past ☐   20 past ☐   25 past ☐

3. Join each shape to its name.

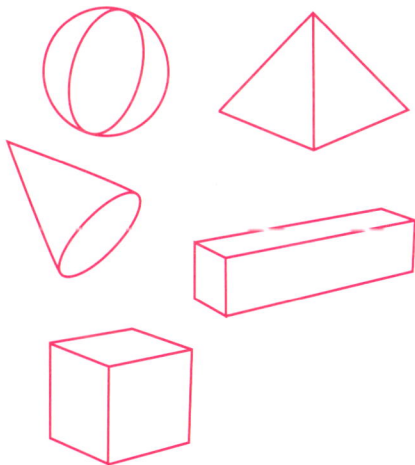

cylinder

cuboid

cone

pyramid

sphere

cube

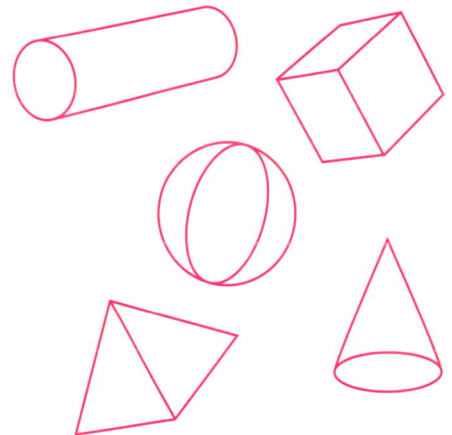

4. Use the digits to write the smallest number.

7, 3 ◯   2, 1 ◯   8, 4 ◯   9, 1 ◯

0, 3 ◯   6, 2 ◯   1, 7 ◯   4, 0 ◯

5. Colour the even numbers.

1. Estimate the length of the lines.

☐ cm   ☐ cm   ☐ cm

☐ cm   ☐ cm   ☐ cm

2. This 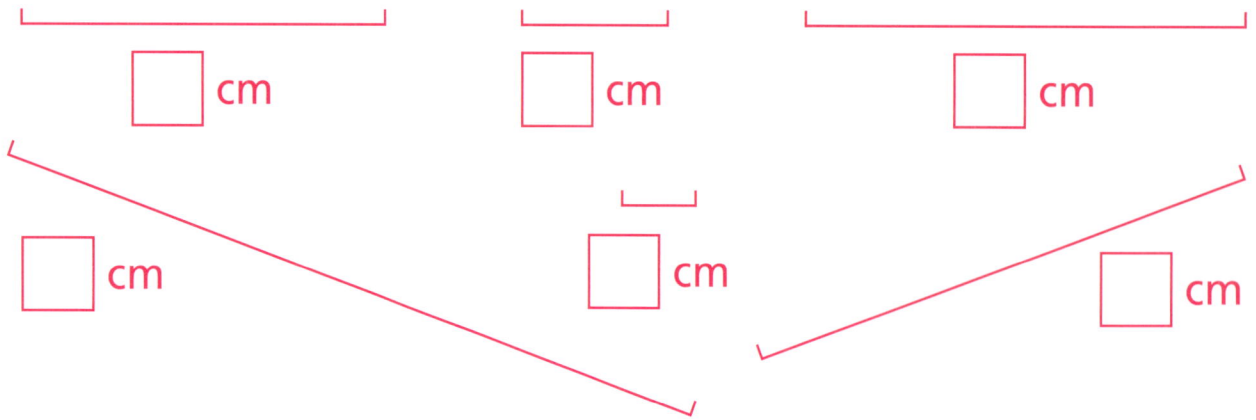 pear costs 10p.

   How much would you pay for...?

   2 pears = ☐ p   6 pears = ☐ p   9 pears = ☐ p

3. Subtract

   60 – 30 = ☐   80 – 20 = ☐   50 – 40 = ☐

   40 – 10 = ☐   90 – 10 = ☐   70 – 30 = ☐

   80 – 40 = ☐   30 – 30 = ☐   100 – 10 = ☐

4. Draw the hands on the clocks.

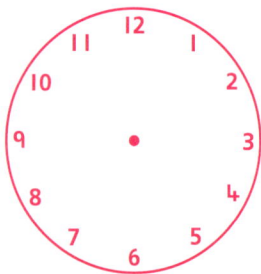   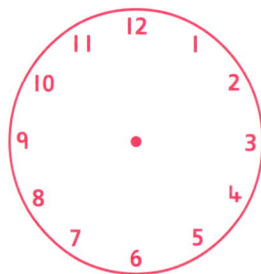   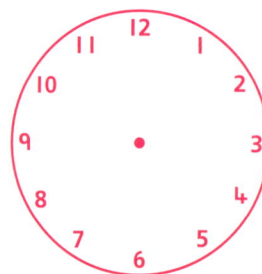   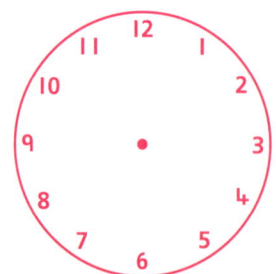

   20 past 2   25 past 11   20 past 12   25 past 7

5. Write 1 less and 1 more than each number.

   ☐ (15) ☐   ☐ (28) ☐   ☐ (39) ☐   ☐ (60) ☐

Progress Test D

1. Estimate how long each snake is.

 ☐ cm   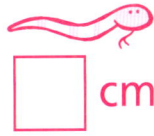 ☐ cm

 ☐ cm

2. Add

23 + 27 = ☐   42 + 54 = ☐

41 + 35 = ☐   68 + 11 = ☐

29 + 20 = ☐   82 + 17 = ☐

3. Draw the hands on the clocks.

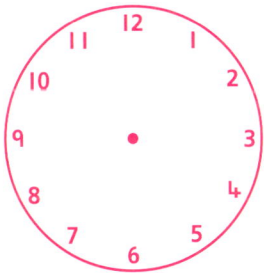   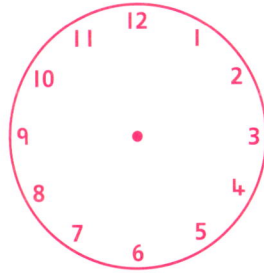

20 past 12   25 past 5

4. Write the next even number.

4 ☐   0 ☐   8 ☐

6 ☐   2 ☐   10 ☐

5. Name the month before

June _____   December _____

May _____   July _____

September _____

6. Join the pairs of beetles that add up to 60.

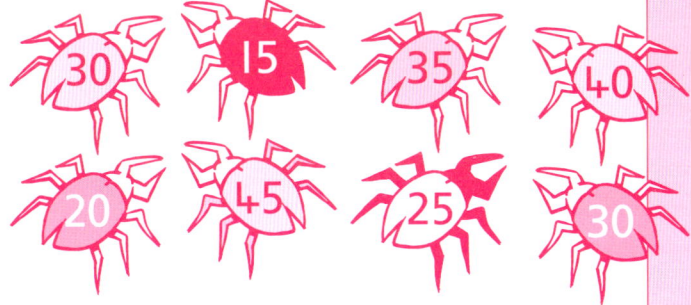

7. Write 1 less than the number and 1 more.

8. Subtract

28 – 10 = ☐   37 – 17 = ☐

42 – 21 = ☐   59 – 18 = ☐

68 – 34 = ☐   79 – 41 = ☐

9. How much more to make 75p?

☐ p   ☐ p   ☐ p

10. Draw a big sphere and a small sphere.

Name something that is a sphere.

_____

19

1. Find 3 numbers to add up to the number in each triangle.

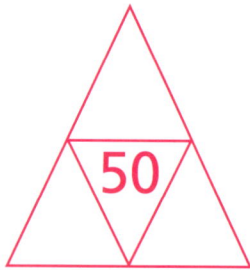

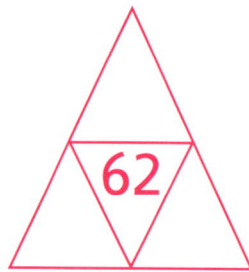

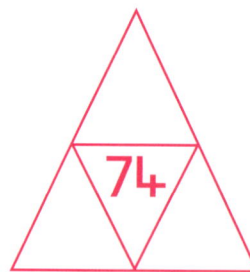

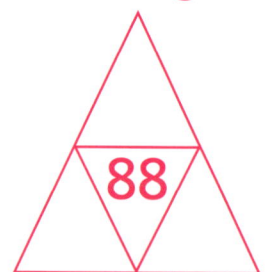

△ 50   △ 62   △ 74   △ 88

2. Count in 5s.

(5)(10)( )( )( )( )( )( )( )( )( )

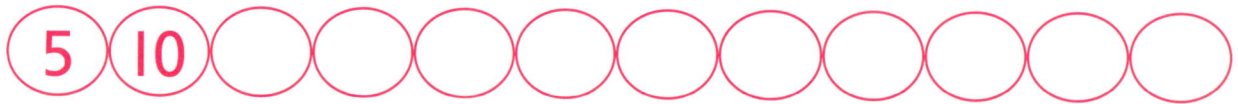

3. Animals at the farm.

cows
hens
horses
sheep
ducks

| | 1 | 2 | 3 | 4 | 5 | 6 | 7 | 8 | 9 | 10 |

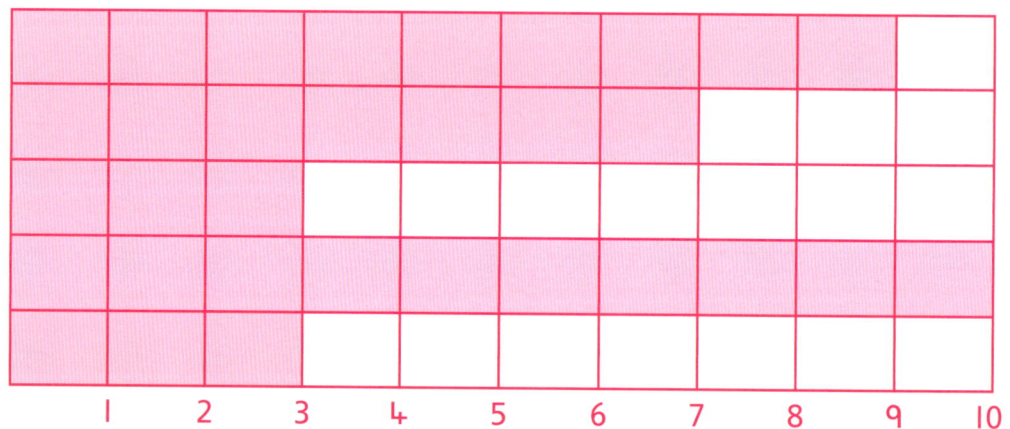

There are ☐ horses   ☐ sheep   ☐ cows

There are ☐ more sheep than ducks

There are ☐ more hens than horses

How many animals are there altogether? ☐

4. Subtract

$39 - 19 = $ ☐ $47 - 23 = $ ☐ $55 - 35 = $ ☐

$64 - 30 = $ ☐ $79 - 61 = $ ☐ $82 - 12 = $ ☐

$92 - 70 = $ ☐ $50 - 25 = $ ☐ $100 - 98 = $ ☐

5. 10 more than.

29 ⬡   17 ⬡   32 ⬡   69 ⬡   84 ⬡   79 ⬡

1. Fill in the missing numbers.

25 + △ = 50   32 + △ = 65   55 + △ = 66

48 + △ = 69   78 + △ = 87   62 + △ = 76

△ + 23 = 34   △ + 41 = 68   △ + 22 = 96

2. Which coins can you use to buy?

 27p    15p    30p    56p

3. Write the time.

      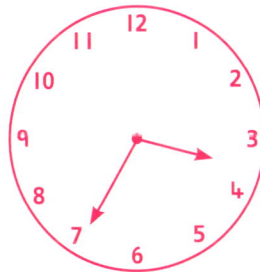   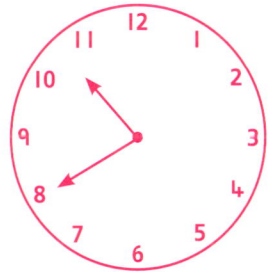

☐ to ☐   ☐ to ☐   ☐ to ☐   ☐ to ☐

4. 10 less than.

15 ⬡   37 ⬡   29 ⬡   52 ⬡   48 ⬡   67 ⬡

5. Write these numbers in order starting with the smallest.

_____ _____ _____ _____ _____ _____

1. Circle the digit in each number that shows the tens.

26 16 39 52 84 91

2. Count in 5s. Fill in the missing numbers.

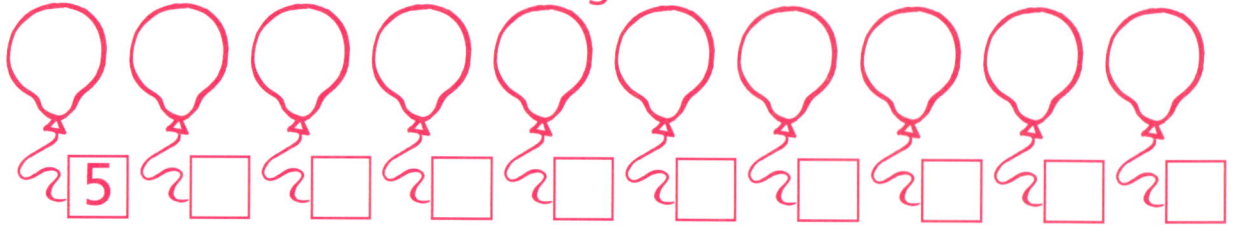

5 | | | | | | | | |

3. Finish the bills.

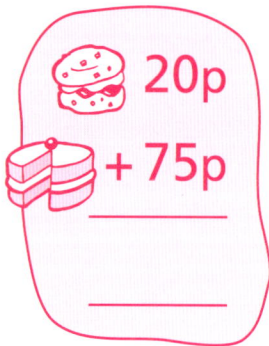

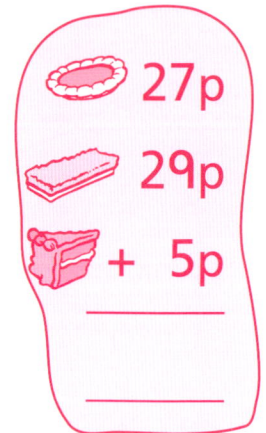

20p
+ 75p
_____
_____

25p
+ 14p
_____
_____

35p
+ 25p
_____
_____

27p
29p
+ 5p
_____
_____

4. Add and Take

29 + 10 − 9 = ☐   32 + 16 − 18 = ☐   36 + 18 − 14 = ☐

42 + 20 − 11 = ☐   56 + 14 − 25 = ☐   62 + 15 − 13 = ☐

65 + 15 − 20 = ☐   81 + 15 − 12 = ☐   76 + 18 − 16 = ☐

5.

Tom had 27 conkers and Finn found 21 conkers.

How many conkers did they have altogether? ☐

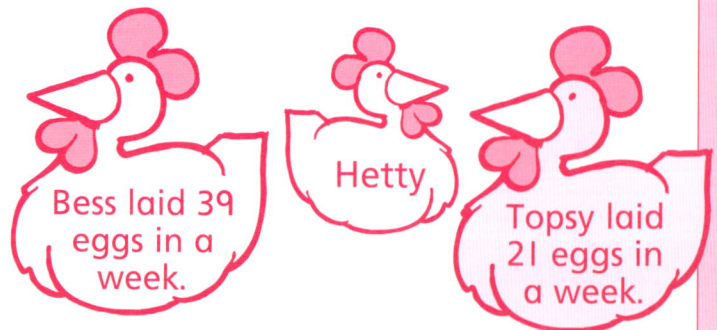

Bess laid 39 eggs in a week.

Hetty

Topsy laid 21 eggs in a week.

How many eggs did Bess and Topsy together lay in a week? ☐

How many more eggs does Hetty have to lay to give the farmer 75 eggs? ☐

Progress Test E

1. Continue the pattern.

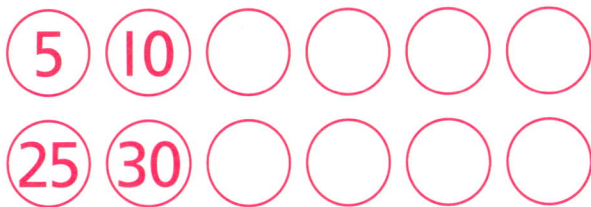

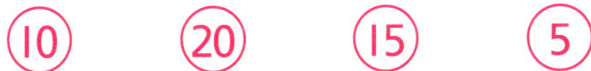

2. Use these numbers to make your own sums and answers.

⑩   ⑳   ⑮   ⑤

☐ + ☐ = ☐   ☐ − ☐ = ☐

☐ + ☐ = ☐   ☐ − ☐ = ☐

3. Draw as many ways as you can to pay for this kite.

26p

4. Colour the odd numbers.

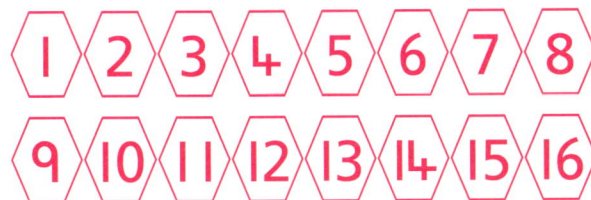

5. Make 75p in each group.

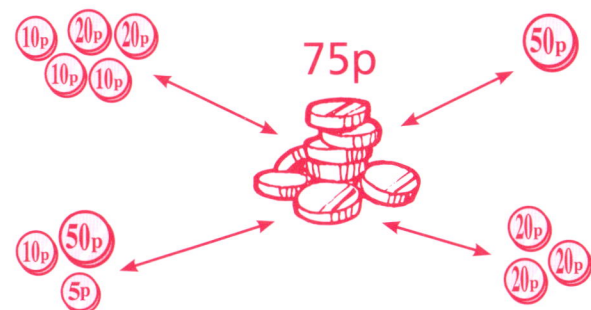

6. How many of each coin to make £1?

☐ 50p   ☐ 20p   ☐ 10p

7. How many 10s in…?

40 ◯   49 ◯   26 ◯

85 ◯   38 ◯   92 ◯

8. How much change?

30p − 25p = ☐   35p − 15p = ☐

50p − 29p = ☐   40p − 12p = ☐

29p − 19p = ☐   32p − 16p = ☐

9. Draw the hands on the clocks.

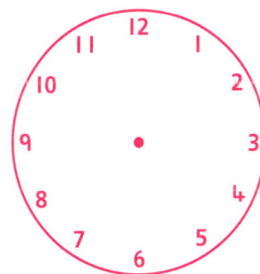 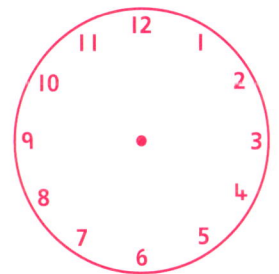

20 to 10   25 to 12

10. Add 5 to each number.

1. **What can you buy?**

For   30p _____   45p _____

50p _____   75p _____

If you bought a trowel and a tulip how much change would you have from 50p? ☐ p

2. **Multiply**

2 x 5 = ☐   6 x 5 = ☐   4 x 5 = ☐

5 x 5 = ☐   3 x 5 = ☐   8 x 5 = ☐

7 x 5 = ☐   10 x 5 = ☐   9 x 5 = ☐

3.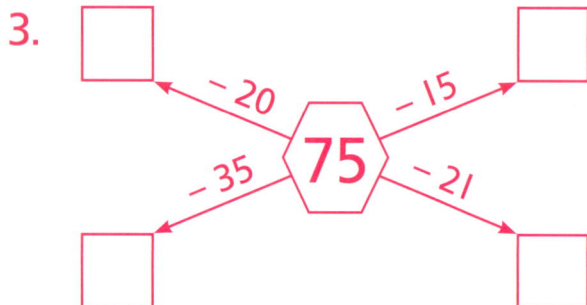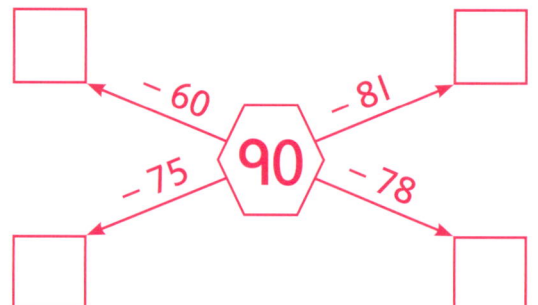

4. **Join the numbers to their nearest 10.**

49   21

15   29

17         32

42   47

5. **Colour the shapes that have at least one right angle.**

  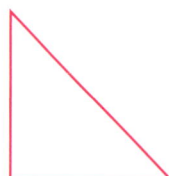 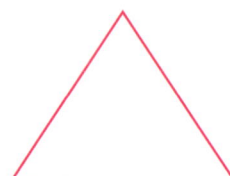 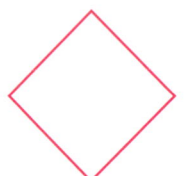

1. Double the numbers.

25 = ☐   15 = ☐   42 = ☐

24 = ☐   33 = ☐   50 = ☐

2. Colour the odd numbers with a red crayon.
   Colour the even numbers with a blue crayon.

(10) (1) (2) (3) (4) (5) (11) (13) (18)
(12)   (20) 8
(7) (6) (19) (16) (17) (14) (9) (15)

3. Adding and Taking

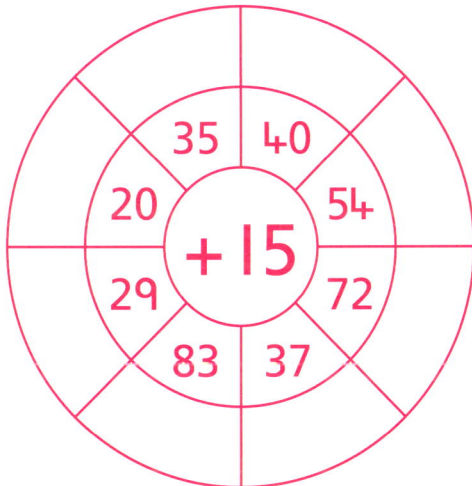

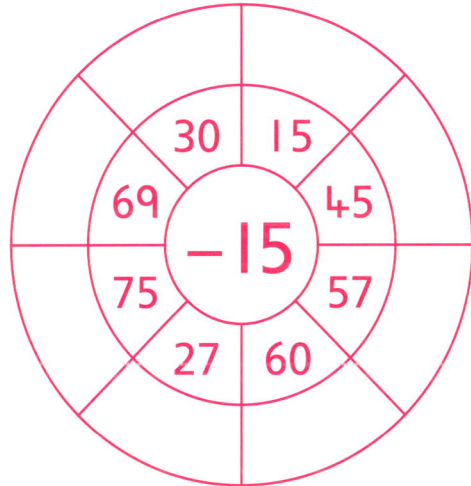

35	40
20	+15	54
29		72
83	37

30	15
69	−15	45
75		57
27	60

4. Use + or − signs to make the answers correct.

54 ⟩ + 10 ⟨ 64   39 ⟩ 20 ⟨ 59   63 ⟩ 9 ⟨ 72

48 ⟩ 8 ⟨ 56   96 ⟩ 12 ⟨ 84   76 ⟩ 11 ⟨ 87

5. Write these numbers in order starting with the largest.

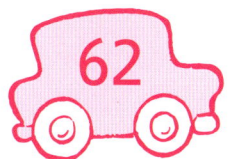

38   26   74   97   62

○   ○   ○   ○   ○

1. Colour the pentagons.

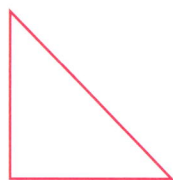  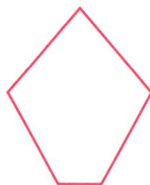  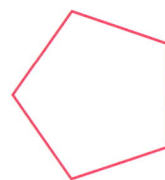 

2.  35p  30p  16p 30p  TEA  SOUP 23p  18p

Buy and show how much change you would get from 75p.

	Cost	Change		Cost	Change
			 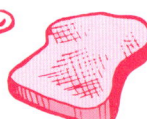		

3. Show the time on the digital clock.

     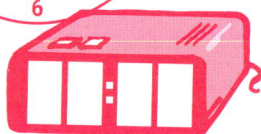    

4. Find $\frac{1}{2}$ of the following numbers.

6 ☐   4 ☐   8 ☐   12 ☐

10 ☐   14 ☐   20 ☐   16 ☐

5. Find the total of 9 and 32 ⬭   Add 15 and 42 ⬭

16 plus 8 ⬭   What is the sum of 29 and 11? ⬭

Progress Test F

1. Write the time.

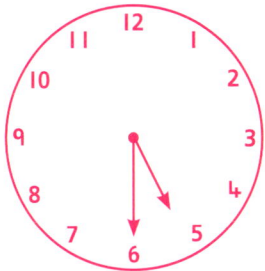

2. Write down all the odd numbers less than 20.

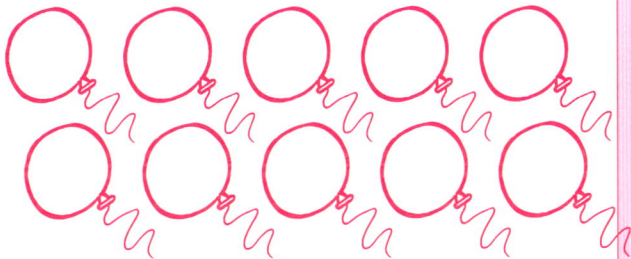

3. Draw 2 coins to make each amount.

   55p

   70p

   £1

4. 10 less than.

   17 △   33 △   59 △

   84 △   98 △   90 △

5. Draw a shape with 4 right angles.

6. Fill in the missing numbers.

   29 + ☐ = 40   17 + ☐ = 34

   73 + ☐ = 87   39 + ☐ = 52

   82 + ☐ = 99   55 + ☐ = 80

7. Write the nearest 10.

   37 ⬡   18 ⬡   42 ⬡

   11 ⬡   99 ⬡   73 ⬡

   55 ⬡   92 ⬡   89 ⬡

8. Draw a pentagon.

9. How much more?

   Tom had 50p.
   How much more did he need to buy...?

   57p ☐ p   65p ☐ p

   76p ☐ p   62p ☐ p

10. Multiply

   6 x 5 = ☐   8 x 5 = ☐

   10 x 5 = ☐   3 x 5 = ☐

   4 x 5 = ☐   9 x 5 = ☐

1. Write all the odd numbers between 50 and 70.

2. Look at these objects and join them to the solid shape they are most like.

    cuboid

cube

cylinder

sphere

3. Use two of these numbers in the shapes to add up to 76.

51 16 34 60 25 42

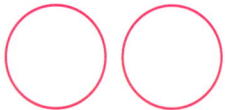   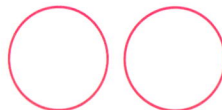   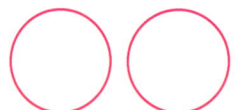

Use two of these numbers in the shapes to add up to 94.

33 70 42 24 61 52

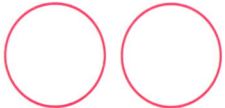   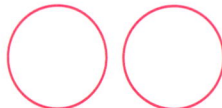   

4. Draw the lines of symmetry.

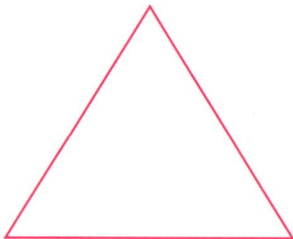      

5. Circle all the numbers which lie between 50 and 70.

15	25	56	71	17	5	46	52	75	65
35	64	61	51	60	36	27	16	53	48
72	69	62	6	5	59	54	66	71	45
57	63	58	76	68	49	85	96	55	67

1. Write in the even numbers from 82.

2. Find the total of 29 and 31 ☐   25 add 75 = ☐

   Added together 45 and 52 make ☐

   38 plus 61 makes ☐   40 more than 56 = ☐

3. Make the coins in each group add up to £1.

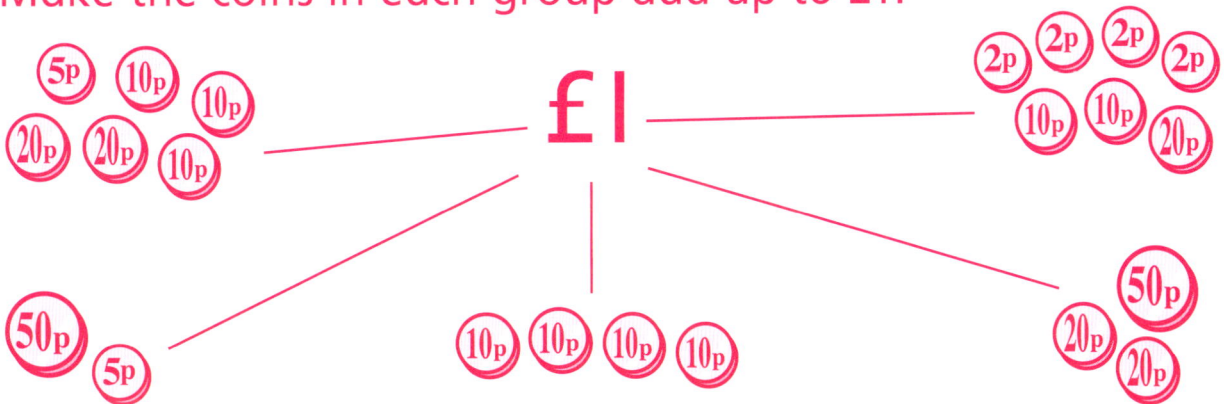

4. Start at 29   Start at 72

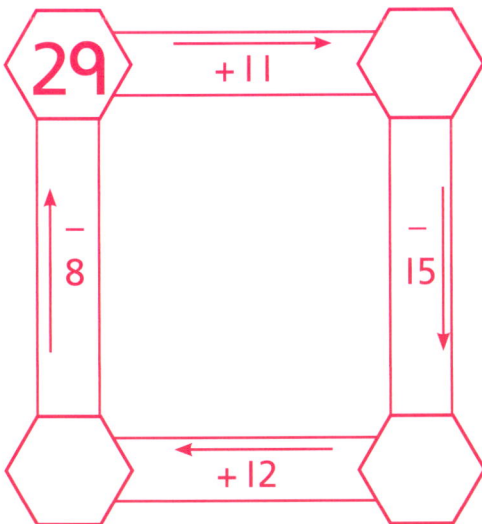
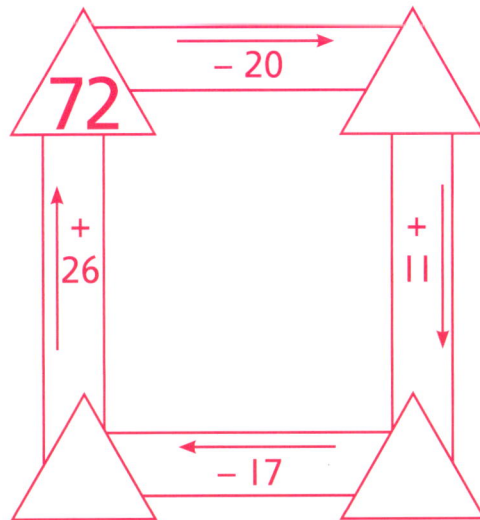

5. Colour the shapes that have curved edges.

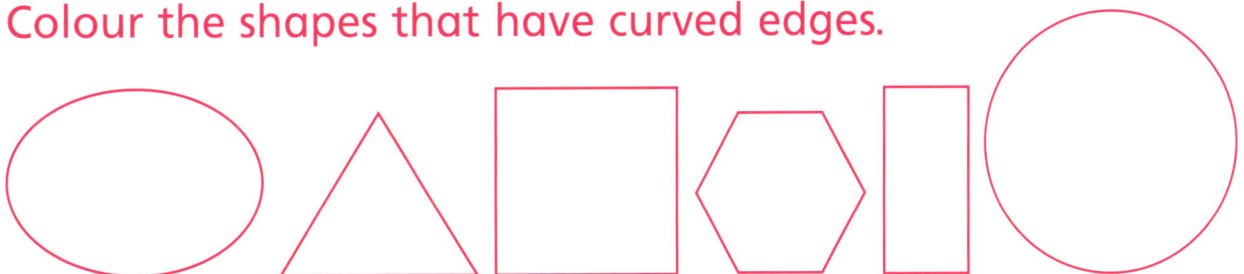

1. Multiply by 2

8 x 2 = ☐   5 x 2 = ☐   9 x 2 = ☐

6 x 2 = ☐   10 x 2 = ☐   4 x 2 = ☐

3 x 2 = ☐   7 x 2 = ☐   2 x 2 = ☐

2. Subtract 25 from 35 ☐   Take 18 from 99 ☐

Find the difference between 54 and 33 = ☐

78 minus 52 = ☐   87 take away 47 = ☐

3. Buy 2 of each.

4p ⬡   8p ⬡   10p ⬡

7p ⬡   9p ⬡   6p ⬡

4. How many faces does each shape have?

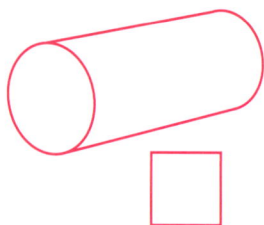

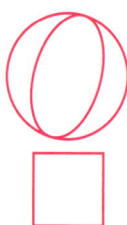

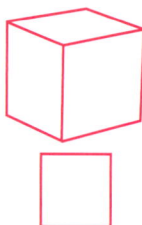

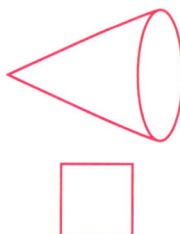

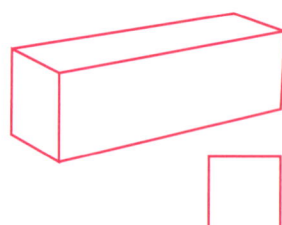

☐   ☐   ☐   ☐   ☐

5. Draw lines to join pairs of numbers that add up to 100.

50   75   50   36   25

18   64   82   43   57

Puzzle Page

Write the answers in words.

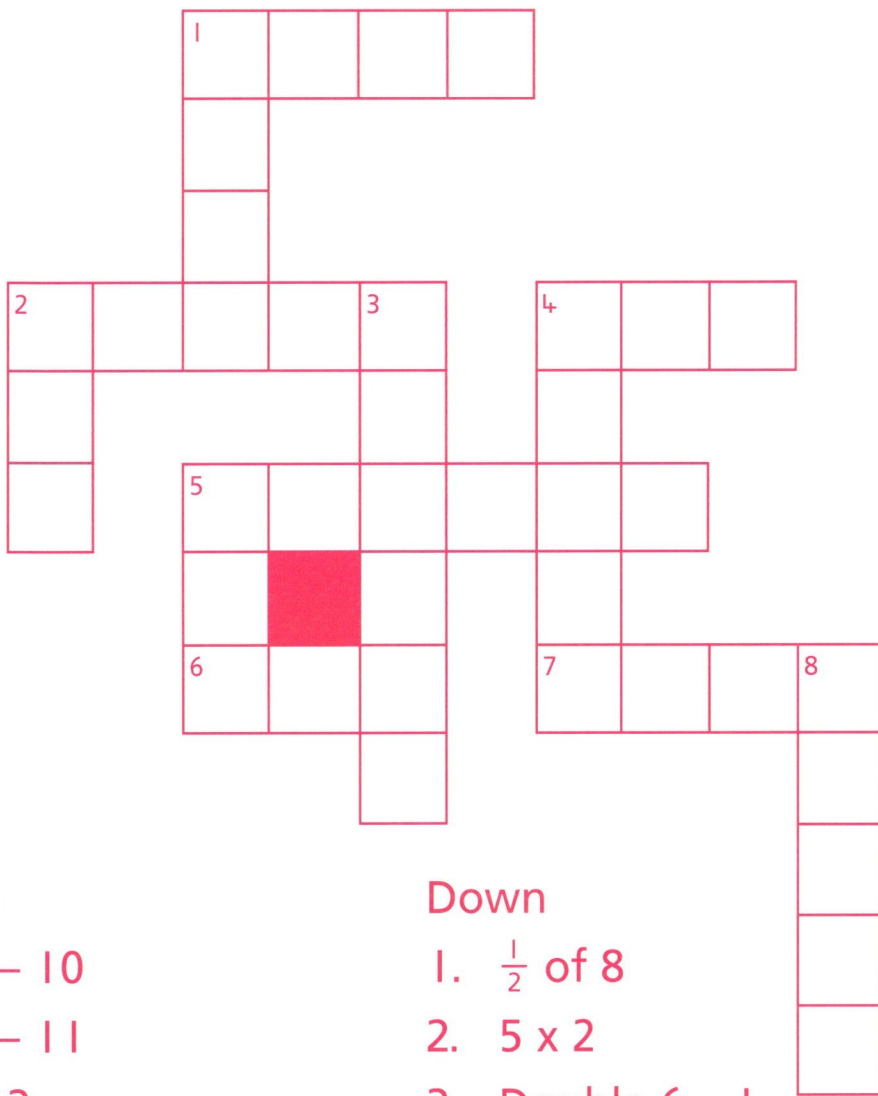

Across

1. 15 − 10
2. 14 − 11
4. 3 x 2
5. 13 + 6 − 7
6. 50 − 49
7. 20 − 11

Down

1. $\frac{1}{2}$ of 8
2. 5 x 2
3. Double 6 − 1
4. $\frac{1}{2}$ of 14
5. Number of faces on a cone
8. Double 4

one two three five seven nine eleven

four six eight ten twelve

Schofield & Sims

the long-established educational publisher specialising in maths, English and science

The series **Mental Maths** develops children's ability to understand number problems and to use their knowledge to resolve these problems confidently and logically.

Mental Maths Book 2 covers:

- Counting and ordering numbers to 100
- Patterns and sequences
- Counting money and calculating change
- 2-D and 3-D shapes
- Tens and units, addition and subtraction of two-digit numbers
- Time problems
- Estimating and measuring
- Multiples of 2, 5 and 10.

The full range of titles in the series is as follows:

Mental Maths Book 1:	ISBN 978 07217 0962 8
Mental Maths Book 2:	ISBN 978 07217 0963 5

Have you tried **Problem Solving** by Schofield & Sims?
This series of books helps children to sharpen their mathematical skills by applying their knowledge to 'real-life' situations, such as shopping and telling the time.

For further information and to place your order visit www.schofieldandsims.co.uk or telephone 01484 607080

FSC
MIX
Paper from responsible sources
FSC® C023114

ISBN 978-07217-0963-5

Schofield & Sims

7 Mariner Court, Wakefield, West Yorkshire WF4 3FL, UK
Phone: 01484 607080 Facsimile: 01484 606815
E-mail: sales@schofieldandsims.co.uk
www.schofieldandsims.co.uk

9 780721 709635

ISBN 978 07217 0963 5

£4.95 (Retail price)

Key Stage 1

Age range 5-7 years